Five Short Shorts
American short stories

Five Short Shorts

American short stories

edited by Günter Kaymer

Ernst Klett Sprachen
Stuttgart

1. Auflage   1   16 15 14 13 12 | 2027 26 25 24 23

Nachfolger von 978-3-549600-2
Alle Drucke dieser Auflage sind unverändert und können im Unterricht nebeneinander verwendet werden.
Die letzte Zahl bezeichnet das Jahr des Druckes. Das Werk und seine Teile sind urheberrechtlich geschützt. Jede Nutzung in anderen als den gesetzlich zugelassenen Fällen bedarf der vorherigen schriftlichen Einwilligung des Verlags.

Edited by Günter Kaymer
Layoutkonzeption: Elmar Feuerbach
Gestaltung und Satz: Satz & mehr, Besigheim
Umschlaggestaltung: Elmar Feuerbach
Titelbild: Wolfgang Volz, Stuttgart
Druck und Bindung: Digitaldruck Tebben GmbH, Biessenhofen

Printed in Germany
ISBN 978-3-12-549601-9

Contents

1. Ruthless

by William DeMille

Outside, the woods lay in clear October sunlight; the autumn air was full of the sharp, exciting smell of
5 moist, leaf-covered earth. Inside, a man smiled grimly as he turned from the bathroom cabinet, entered the primitive living-room of his mountain camp, and crossed to a closet set in the pine wall.

It was his special closet with a spring lock, and in it
10 he kept guns, ammunition, fishing-rods, and liquor. Not even his wife was allowed to have a key, for Judson Webb loved his personal possessions and became furious if they were touched by any hand but his own.

15 The closet door stood open; he had been packing his things away for the winter, and in a few minutes he would be driving back to civilization.

As he looked at the shelf on which the liquor stood, his smile was not attractive. All the bottles were
20 unopened except one quart of Bourbon which was placed invitingly in front, a whiskey glass by its side. This bottle was less than half full. As he took it from the shelf, his wife spoke from the next bedroom. "Everything is packed, Judson," she said. "Hasn't Alec
25 come to turn the water off and get the keys?"

Alec lived about a mile down the road and acted as caretaker for the city folks when they were away.

---

1 **ruthless** [ˈruːθlɪs] cruel, pitiless – 5 **moist** [mɔɪst] damp, wet – 5 **grimly** in an unpleasant, unfriendly way – 8 **closet** [ˈklɒzɪt] *(AE)* small cupboard – 8 **set** fixed – 8 **pine** [paɪn] kind of evergreen tree – 9 **spring lock** [ˈsprɪŋˈlɒk] door lock that jumps back automatically – 10 **fishing-rod** long, thin stick of wood or metal to catch fish with – 10 **liquor** [ˈlɪkə] alcoholic drinks – 12 **Judson Webb** [ˈdʒʌdsn ˈweb] name – 13 **furious** [ˈfjʊəriəs] very angry – 20 **quart** [kwɔːt] the fourth part of a gallon = about one litre – 20 **Bourbon** [ˈbɜːbən] kind of American whiskey – 24 **Alec** [ˈælɪk] short for Alexander [ˌælɪɡˈzɑːndə] – 27 **caretaker** [ˈkeəteikə] sb who looks after a building, who takes care of it – 27 **folks** [fəʊks] people

"He's down at the lake taking the boats out of the water. He said he'd be back in half an hour."

Mabel came into the room carrying her suitcase. But she paused in surprise as she saw the bottle in 5 her husband's hand. "Judson!" she exclaimed, "You're not taking a drink at ten o'clock in the morning, are you?"

"You're wrong, my dear," he chuckled, "I'm not taking anything out of this bottle; I'm only putting 10 something into it." His closed hand opened, and he put two tiny white tablets on the table as he started to uncork the whiskey.

Her eyes narrowed as she watched him. She had learned to dread that tone of his voice; it was the tone 15 he used when he was planning to 'put something over' in business.

"Whoever broke into my closet last winter and stole my liquor will probably try it again once we are out of here," he went on, "only this time he'll wish he 20 hadn't."

She caught her breath at his cruel vindictiveness as one by one he dropped the tablets into the bottle and held it up to watch them dissolve.

"What are they?" she asked, "something to make 25 him sick?"

"And how!" He seemed fascinated as he saw the Bourbon changing into a deadly drink.

"At least no one has found an antidote: once it's down, it's the end."

30 He corked the bottle and set it back on the shelf alongside the little whiskey glass. "Everything nice

---

3 **Mabel** ['meɪbl] Mrs. Webb's Christian name – 8 **to chuckle** ['tʃʌkl] to laugh with a closed mouth – 11 **tiny** ['taɪnɪ] very small – 14 **to dread** [dred] to fear – 16 **to put sth over** *here*: to carry out one's plans dishonestly – 21 **vindictiveness** [vɪn'dɪktɪvnəs] desire for revenge, cruelty – 26 **fascinated** ['fæsɪneɪtɪd] hypnotized – 28 **antidote** ['æntɪdəʊt] medicine used against a poison

and handy," he remarked, "now, Mr. Thief, when you break in, have a good drink; I won't begrudge you this one."

The woman's face was pale. "Don't do it, Judson," she gasped, "it's horrible – it's murder."

"The law doesn't call it murder if I shoot a thief who is entering my house by force," he said harshly. "Also, the use of rat poison is not forbidden. The only way any rat can get into this closet is to break in. What happens then has nothing to do with me."

"Don't do it, Judson," she begged, "the law doesn't punish burglary by death; so what right have you ...?"

"When it comes to protecting my property, I make my own laws." His deep voice was like that of a big dog growling at the possible loss of a bone.

"But all they did was to steal a little liquor," she pleaded, "probably some boys off on a lark. They didn't do any real damage."

"That's not the point," he said. "If a man holds me up and robs me of five dollars, it makes me just as sore as if he took a hundred. A thief's a thief."

She made one last effort. "We won't be here till next spring. I can't bear to think of that death-trap waiting there all the time. Suppose something happens to us – and no one knows ..." He chuckled once more at her words. "We'll take a chance on that," he said, "I've made my pile by taking chances. If I should die, you can do as you please. The stuff will be yours."

---

2 **to begrudge sb sth** [bɪˈɡrʌdʒ] to object if sb does sth – 5 **to gasp** [ɡɑːsp] to take short breaths when speaking quickly – 7 **harshly** [ˈhɑːʃlɪ] in a cold and cruel way – 12 **burglary** [ˈbɜːɡlərɪ] breaking into houses and stealing things – 16 **to growl** [ɡraʊl] to make low sounds like dogs when they are angry – 18 **to plead** [pliːd] *here:* to ask earnestly, to speak in favour of sb – 18 **to be off on a lark** to do sth for fun, to play a joke on sb – 22 **sore** [sɔː] *(AE) here:* angry – 23 **effort** [ˈefət] try, attempt – 24 **death-trap** [ˈdeθtræp] thing which may kill sb – 28 **to make one's pile** [paɪl] to become rich, to be successful in business – 28 **to take a chance on sth** [tʃɑːnts] to risk sth; to take things as they come

It was useless to argue – she knew. He had always been ruthless in business and whenever anything crossed him. Things had to be done his way. She turned toward the door with a sigh.

5   "I'll walk down the road and say good-bye at the farm house," she said quietly, "you can pick me up there." She had made up her mind to tell Alec's wife. Someone had to know.

  "Okay, my dear," he smiled, "and don't worry about
10 your poor little burglar. No one is going to get hurt who hasn't got it coming to him."

  As she went down the path, he started to close the closet door, then paused as he remembered his hunting boots outside on the porch. They belonged
15 in the closet.

  So leaving the door open, he went to fetch them from the heavy, rustic table on which they stood, along with his bag and top coat.

  Alec was coming up from the lake and waved to him
20 from a distance.

  A chipmunk, hearing Judson's heavy tread, left the acorn it was about to add to its store within the cabin wall and disappeared.

  When reaching for his boots, Judson stepped upon
25 that acorn. His foot slid from under him and his head struck the massive table as he fell.

  Several minutes later, he began to regain his senses. Alec's strong arm was supporting his head as he lay on the porch, and a kindly voice was saying, "It wasn't

---

4 **sigh** [saɪ] deep breath which shows sadness – 11 **who hasn't got it coming to him** who is not to blame for it himself, who doesn't deserve it – 12 **path** [pɑːθ] narrow way through fields and woods – 14 **porch** [pɔːtʃ] the roofed entrance of a building – 17 **rustic table** ['rʌstik] rough, massive table like country-people often have – 21 **chipmunk** ['tʃɪpmʌŋk] small tree-animal with a bushy tail – 21 **tread** [tred] step – 22 **acorn** ['eɪkɔːn] fruit of an oak tree – 25 **to slide** [slaɪd] **(slid, slid)** [slɪd] to glide, to move away – 26 **to strike** [straɪk] **(struck, struck)** [strʌk] to hit sth, to fall against sth – 27 **to regain one's senses** [rɪ'geɪn] to be able to think again

much of a fall, Mr. Webb. You ain't cut none; just knocked out for a minute. Here, take this. It'll pull you together."

A small whiskey glass was pressed to Judson's lips.
5 Dazed and half-conscious, he drank.

1 **you ain't cut none** [eɪnt] *(AE, slang)* you are not hurt, nothing is broken – 5 **dazed** [deɪzd] unable to think clearly – 5 **half-conscious** [ˈkɒntʃəs] half-awake

Discuss the following questions:

1. *Is everybody free to do what he likes in his own house? Give reasons for your answer.*
2. *Would you say that Mr. Webb had a good reason for poisoning his liquor?*
3. *What would you have done in this case in order to stop a thief from stealing that liquor?*
4. *What do we learn about Mr. and Mrs. Webb's characters?*
5. *How does a person like Mr. Webb succeed in business life?*
6. *Mr. Webb says, "When it comes to protecting my property, I make my own laws". Do you agree with him?*
7. *Can we speak of the 'irony of fate' with regard to the end of the story? Give your reasons.*
8. *What would you have done that morning if you were Mrs. Webb?*
9. *Do you agree with Mr. Webb that "No one is going to get hurt who hasn't got it coming to him"? Give your reason.*

Question 7 **irony** [ˈaɪərəni] the expression of one's meaning by the direct opposite **fate** power which controls all events and cannot be resisted **irony of fate** event, caused by fate, the exact opposite of what sb wanted to happen

2. The Payoff

by Paul Jones

It was still early, but the morning was so hot that the three men mounting the steep road raised a cloud of white dust that powdered their uniforms and covered their sweaty faces. With the war as good as over, except for the final cleanup, they were heading for the sea in order to escape.

"We ought to be able to get a fishing boat to smuggle us across," said Carter. He was a short, compact man with a bullet head.

"Sure," Lockett agreed, his large, good-humoured face calm, "it'll be a cinch."

"I'm not so certain of that," Hill objected. He set his mouth. "They'll want to be paid, of course. And we haven't any money at all."

"We'll manage it some way," Carter said confidently. "God! It's going to seem funny – going back! Paris and then New York and the old grind again. What were you before you came over, Hill?"

"History instructor and games master in a small prep school," said Hill.

"I was a lawyer," Carter went on, "and what about you, Lockett?"

"Truck-driver," Lockett answered amiably, "pretty much what I did here. Only I won't have anybody shooting at me."

---

1 **payoff** ['peɪɒf] *(AE)* time when wages are paid, *here*: reward – 7 **final cleanup** ['kli:nʌp] *here:* the last war actions, the last battles – 7 **to head for a place** to go in the direction of a place, to move towards a place – 9 **to smuggle sb out** [smʌgl] to take sb out of the country secretly – 10 **Carter** ['kɑːtə] name – 11 **bullet head** ['bʊlɪt] small, round head – 12 **Lockett** ['lɒkɪt] name – 13 **cinch** [sɪntʃ] *(AE) here:* no problem, child's play – 14 **to object** [əb'dʒekt] to disagree, to be against sth – 17 **confidently** ['kɒnfɪdentli] *here:* hopefully – 19 **grind** [graɪnd] *here:* everyday life and work – 20 **Hill** name – 22 **prep school** [prep] private school preparing children for higher education – 23 **lawyer** ['lɔːjə] sb who has studied law – 25 **truck-driver** *(AE)* lorry-driver – 25 **amiably** ['eɪmiəbli] in a friendly way – 26 **pretty much** ['prɪti 'mʌtʃ] *(slang)* almost the same

At about noon they came to the top of a rise and looked down on a village. In the first house an old man gave them a glass of wine.

"I am alone here," he told them, "except for the
5 women and children. I do not know what we shall do for food. All our men are dead or wounded, the 301st battalion – perhaps you have heard of them? All gone," he repeated. "They were fighting just down the road in defence of their village."

10 When the three men went on, the road began to climb into the low hills separating them from the sea. In a ditch they saw a staff car lying on its side. When they peered through the windows, they saw that an officer and his driver were lying dead on the front
15 seat.

"We should have a look in the car and see if they've got anything in there that could be useful for us," Lockett suggested practically.

The loot was two pistols and a flat steel box. When
20 they broke the lock, they saw that it was full of money. A paper with a list of names was headed "301st Battalion."

"A paymaster," Hill said.

"Yeah," said Lockett, "Bringing this sugar up to the
25 guys the old man was talking about. Tough on them – getting knocked off just before payday."

Carter was holding the box, and now he closed the lid and smiled.

"This makes things different," he said.

---

1 **rise** [raɪz] small hill – 12 **ditch** a narrow channel at the side of a road to carry off water – 12 **staff car** [stɑːf] a car for the leading officers of an army – 13 **to peer** to look sharply – 18 **to suggest** [səˈdʒest] to bring forth an idea, to propose – 19 **loot** *here*: things that soldiers find and take away in times of war – 21 **the paper was headed with …** [ˈhedɪd] at the top of the paper was written … – 23 **paymaster** [ˈpeɪmɑːstə] an officer who pays the soldiers – 24 **yeah** [jeə] *(slang)* yes – 24 **sugar** [ˈʃʊgə] *(AE, slang)* money – 25 **guys** [gaɪz] *(AE) here*: soldiers – 25 **tough on them** [[tʌf] *(slang)* they had bad luck – 26 **to be knocked off** [ˈnɒktˈof] *(slang)* to be killed – 28 **lid** cover of a box

"Fifteen thousand odd," he said finally, "there's plenty to take us all the way home."

Hill rubbed his jaw. "I was wondering," he began, "whether we have a right to keep this money."

Carter looked at him. "Wait a minute," he protested, "I'm a lawyer. Whose money is it – if it isn't ours? The government's? It can't be because the government no longer exists. Am I right?"

Hill considered the legal aspects and looked interested but critical.

"Unless," Carter went on ironically, "You think we ought to hand it over to the other side as part of the national resources. Well, you are a historian, Hill. Is that customary?"

"No, of course not," Hill said, staring at his shoes. "There is no precedent for that. I was thinking of the men, of the 301st battalion."

"But it was never theirs," Carter argued. "True, they or their families have a claim for back pay. But this particular box of money never passed into their possession. How can you say that it is theirs?"

"Well, I can't," Hill admitted.

"Whose is it then?" Carter asked keenly. "It was lying here, and we came along and found it. No other owner can be proved for it. Hence, it is ours."

"I think you're right," Hill said. "That was very clearly put, Carter. You must be a good lawyer."

"I am," said Carter. "Now that's settled, all we have to do is to divide the …"

---

1 **odd** *here*: and more – 9 **to consider** [kənˈsɪdə] **the legal aspects** [ˈliːgəl] to think about what the law says in such a case – 13 **resources** [rɪˈsɔːsɪz] property, goods – 13 **historian** [hɪsˈtɔːriən] sb who has studied history or writes about it – 14 **is that customary?** [ˈkʌstəməri] is that the usual way? – 16 **precedent** [ˈpresɪdənt] model case, a case that happened earlier – 18 **to argue** [ˈɑːgjuː] to talk for or against sth – 22 **to admit** [ədˈmɪt] to agree, to confess a mistake – 23 **keenly** [ˈkiːnli] sharply, eagerly – 25 **hence** [hents] so, therefore – 28 **settled** [ˈsetəld] done with, finished

But when he turned, the money was gone – and so was Lockett. They caught a last glimpse of him, outlined against the sky on the hill, and then he vanished.

5 Hill couldn't help laughing. "It's so damnably modern. The intellectuals are debating points of law while the man of action is walking off with the loot."

Carter showed his teeth. "I'll show that fellow who 10 is a man of action. Come on, Hill, let's get him."

They started up the road again, but when they had been walking for an hour, Carter stopped. "We're not being smart," he said. "He has doubled back and he'll be heading for the coast ten miles up."

15 Darkness was drawing in as they passed the wrecked staff car on their way back; and when they came to the village there were lights showing in the dusk.

"We could ask the old man," Hill suggested.

"Right," said Carter.

20 When they came near the house they saw that one window was open. Lockett was sitting at the table in plain view, with the money-box under his hand. The old man was sitting opposite him. Both were drinking wine.

25 "The clown couldn't resist stopping for a drink. All right, Hill, follow me in," Carter whispered, and kicked the door open. His gun was in his hand.

Lockett looked at them without moving from his bench. He was drunk.

---

2 **to catch a glimpse of sb** [glɪmps] to see sb for a very short time – 4 **to vanish** ['vænɪʃ] to disappear, to be lost from view – 5 **damnably** ['dæmnəbli] badly, hatefully – 6 **intellectual** [ɪntɪ'lektjuəl] sb with good thinking power – 13 **smart** *here*: clever, intelligent – 13 **to double back** to turn back quickly – 15 **wrecked** [rekt] broken, ruined – 17 **dusk** the time after sunset before it is quite dark – 22 **in plain view** ['pleɪn 'vju:] in a way that everybody could see him – 26 **to whisper** ['wɪspə] to speak without voice, very softly

"Keep still," Carter said. "We want that money-box."

"Help yourself." Lockett gave the box a push, and Hill took it and put it under his arm.

5 "I demand an explanation," the old man said. "What sort of soldiers are you to come and trouble an honourable paymaster under my roof ?"

"Honourable paymaster?" Carter said rudely. "He's nothing but a thief !"

10 "A thief ?" the old man asked dimly. "But I do not understand. He came here this afternoon with his box and paid to all the widows and orphans the money due to the men of the 301st battalion."

There was a pause during which Hill opened the 15 box. "It's empty all right," he told Carter.

Carter lowered his gun slowly and carefully. "You fool!" he said to Lockett.

"Yeah, sure, I know," Lockett grinned. "Sit down and have a drink before we get going again. Sorry I ran 20 away. But I was afraid that if I listened to any more of that smart talk of yours, you'd have me believing it."

---

8 **rudely** ['ru:dli] in a rough and harsh way – 10 **dimly** *here*: not understanding – 13 **due to sb** [dju:] sth which is to be given to sb (to which sb has a right)

Discuss the following questions:

1. *In what part of the world could this World War II story have happened?*
2. *What caused the soldiers' argument?*
3. *Why did the author of this story mention the educational backgrounds of the three men?*
4. *What were the arguments of the 'intellectuals'?*
5. *What would you have done in this case?*
6. *Why did Lockett decide things on his own?*
7. *Would you say that Lockett acted contrary to comradeship or team-spirit?*
8. *Should a difference be made between war-time morality and peace-time morality?*
9. *Why did Lockett get drunk in the old man's house?*
10. *What would you say is the essence of this story?*

Question 3 **education** [edjʊˈkeiʃn] training in school, college, etc –
Question 7 **contrary to** [ˈkɒntrəri] opposite to, against – **team** group of people who play or work together – **team-spirit** thinking of the success of the team and not of oneself – Question 8 **morality** [məˈrælɪti] standards of good behaviour

3. Keepers Finder

by Charles Palmer

The chauffeur pulled the long black car over to the
side of the dusty road, and the elderly gentleman
5 leaned forward to open the door for the two hitch-
hikers. The slim, nervous one with the beady black
eyes sat down on one side of the elderly gentleman,
the large, sleepy one on the other. The elderly
gentleman's hands were folded in his lap. His friendly
10 eyes peered first at one, then at the other.

He broke the silence. "My name is Vandermoor,
gentlemen. And yours?"

The slim, nervous one sat up sharply. "Any relation
to the Vandermoor bank family?"

15 "Yes," said the elderly gentleman, stroking his gray
goatee. "I have that honour – if you call it one."

"Then," said the slim one, "this is your lucky day.
Isn't it, George?"

The big one took his hungry gaze from the passing
20 orange trees long enough to agree, and then turned
back to watching the luscious fruit.

The slim one fixed the elderly gentleman with a
sharp eye. "Have you ever neglected the birthday of
a loved one and spent sleepless nights of regret?" he
25 asked intensely. "Have you ever forgotten an
anniversary and felt ashamed as a result? Have you

---

1 **keepers finder** a saying: 'He who finds it can keep it.' – 3 **chauffeur** [ˈʃəʊfə] man paid
to drive one's car – 6 **hitch-hiker** [ˈhɪtʃhaɪkə] sb who travels by asking car-drivers for a
free ride (for a lift) – 6 **slim** thin – 6 **beady** [ˈbiːdi] *here*: shining, full of life – 9 **lap** the
upper parts of sb's legs (when sitting) – 11 **Vandermoor** [ˈvændəmʊə] name –
13 **relation** [rɪˈleɪʃn] *here*: family connexion – 15 **to stroke** to pass one's hand along
sth – 16 **goatee** [gəʊˈtiː] small beard – 18 **George** [dʒɔːdʒ] name – 19 **gaze** stare –
21 **luscious** [ˈlʌʃəs] sweet, tasty – 24 **regret** [rɪˈgret] feeling of sadness at the loss of sth
or because sth has not been done – 25 **intensely** [ɪnˈtensli] in excitement, sharply –
26 **anniversary** [ænɪˈvɜːsəri] the yearly return of an event (birthday, etc)

ever failed to congratulate a friend on a promotion and got a cold look the next time you met him? Have you?"

"Well, yes," said the elderly gentleman, "I have. I am a little forgetful at times. But then, most people are."

"Ah," the slim one went on, giving the lapel an impressive shake, "this exactly is my point. Most people are, like you, forgetful. And they suffer for it. They suffer because they know the omission was not intended, and they also realize that the neglected one will certainly misunderstand. Maybe a long friendship will be strained, or a wife or daughter hurt."

"But," he went on, "suppose you suddenly find yourself in a position where those omissions will never happen any more! Would you be glad – especially if it meant no effort on your part, no time, in fact nothing except for the payment of a very small fee?"

The elderly gentleman nodded. "I imagine most people would be as delighted as I."

"My point again!" cried the slim one. "Now, George and I are at this moment on our way to Los Angeles to start just such a service. We plan to call it 'The Tell-You-When Co.'. All you have to do is to give us the names of the people whose anniversaries you want to remember with the dates, if you have them. Otherwise we will look them up for you."

"Oh, I see," said the elderly gentleman.

"Give us also," the slim one went on, "the names of those people whose promotions, marriages, births,

---

1 **promotion** [prəˈməʊʃən] moving up to a higher rank – 7 **lapel** [ləˈpel] front part of the collar of a coat – 10 **omission** [əʊˈmɪʃn] forgetting or leaving out things – 13 **to strain** [streɪn] to risk, to weaken, to endanger – 13 **to hurt sb** [hɜːt] **(hurt, hurt)** *here*: to cause pain or sadness to sb – 18 **fee** sum of money one has to pay for a service – 20 **to be delighted** [dɪˈlaɪtɪd] to be very pleased, glad – 22 **Los Angeles** [lɒsˈændʒɪliːz] city in California

deaths, and so on you want to mark with a gift or a note; and our clipping service will watch the papers and other sources of information. When an item appears on the calendar which we keep in your name,

5 we'll notify you, and for a small additional fee we'll even write a suitable note, or buy and send a gift. Now, tell me: does that fill a long-felt need?"

The elderly gentleman's eyes were bright with interest. "Amazing, young man! Exactly what I need.

10 Put me down as your first subscriber."

"You see," said the slim one, "you snapped at it. So will others. Which brings us to the heart of the matter. Doesn't it, George?"

George turned from the oranges long enough to

15 agree a second time, and then he turned back to the window. An orange would be a very fine thing just now.

The slim one grasped the elderly gentleman's lapel again. "Mr. Vandermoor, I called this your lucky day.

20 It is. You, being a Vandermoor, have money which you are probably willing to treble on a proposition that can't miss. George and I have such a proposition, but no money. Now, why can't we get together on this thing?"

25 "Hmm," remarked the elderly gentleman. "How much capital do you think you need for your venture."

---

1 **to mark** to notice, to pay attention to, to make a sign – 2 **to clip** to cut things out (newspaper articles, etc) – 3 **item** ['aitəm] note or mark in a list of names or on a calendar – 5 **to notify** ['nəʊtɪfaɪ] to inform – 9 **amazing** [ə'meɪzɪŋ] wonderful – 10 **subscriber** [səb'skraɪbə] sb paying a certain sum of money for a service which others promise to do for him – 11 **to snap at sth** to see a chance and take it – 18 **to grasp** [grɑːsp] to take sth with a firm hand, to seize – 21 **to treble** [trebl] to make sth three times as much – 21 **proposition** [prɒpə'zɪʃn] *here:* plan, suggestion – 27 **venture** ['ventʃə] risky try, undertaking

The slim one watched him carefully. "Well, there's advertising, office rent, telephones, and living expenses for George and me – all only until the golden flood begins to roll in. Say ... oh, say ... five thousand
5 dollars. That should be enough to start the business."

The elderly gentleman drew a checkbook from his pocket and took his fountain pen. The beady eyes glistened. The elderly gentleman turned to the back
10 of a check and began to figure. The slim one breathed out sharply, opened his mouth to speak, but thought better of it.

In a few moments, the elderly gentleman stopped figuring and looked out of the car window, stroking
15 his goatee thoughtfully. He shook his head slowly.

"No," he said, "I believe your calculations are wrong. You will need at least ten thousand dollars to get your proposition under way."

The blood slowly flowed back into the slim one's
20 cheeks.

Mr. Vandermoor turned his checkbook over. "I am a man of quick decisions," he told the slim one. "I am convinced of your idea and of your ability to carry it through. Your name?"

25 The slim one gave it, and the elderly gentleman wrote out the check, tore it from the book, and handed it to him. "And now I see we are almost home. If you young men will come in with me, we can draw up some papers to cover the matter; and then I will have

---

2 **advertising** ['ædvətaɪzɪŋ] making things known in newspapers etc in order to sell them – 2 **rent** money which must be paid for the use of a building or a room – 4 **flood** [flʌd] *here*: great quantity of money – 4 **say** *here*: let's say – 9 **to glisten** [glɪsn] to sparkle, to shine brightly – 10 **to figure** ['fɪgə] *here*: to calculate and put down figures – 11 **to think better of it** to change one's mind – 18 **to get sth under way** to get sth going – 26 **to tear** [teə] **(tore, torn)** [tɔː tɔːn] to pull sharply, to take sth away by force – 28 **to draw sth up** *here*: to write sth down on paper – 29 **to cover the matter** to settle things, to fix things

my driver take you on to the city to start your company."

The car swung from the highway and stopped smoothly. A uniformed man hobbled from the gate house to unlock the heavy iron gate which barred the driveway.

Suddenly the slim one bent forward. His eyes rested on a small bronze plate in the stone pillar. "Sunnyside Home for the Mentally Diseased," he read slowly – unable to breathe as the words sank in.

He turned toward George with a hopeless glance. George turned away sadly. The slim one's eyes dropped to the attractive signature on the check he was still holding in his hands: "Napoleon Vandermoor," he read. His lips tightened for a moment. Then he grinned sheepishly.

"Okay, Napoleon," he said, "I bet your name isn't Vandermoor. But just to even it up: George and I aren't starting any Tell-You-When Service either! Just because somebody else beat us to it a year ago. All we wanted your dough for was to skip the country before the dicks caught us."

He kissed the check regretfully, then tore it into little pieces and tossed them in the air.

"Come on, George," he said, "oranges for breakfast." The elderly gentleman watched them trudge down the road. He stroked his goatee as the car rolled up the drive.

---

4 **smoothly** [smuːðli] without shaking or bumping – 4 **to hobble** [hɒbl] to walk as if lame – 8 **bronze** [brɒnz] a metal; a mixture of copper and tin – 8 **plate** *here*: flat piece of metal – 8 **pillar** ['pɪlə] post as part of the gate – 9 **mentally** diseased ['mentəli dɪ'ziːzd] people who are unable to think clearly, insane or mad people – 14 **Napoleon** [nə'pəʊlɪən] Christian name – 15 **to tighten** ['taɪtən] to draw together – 16 **sheepishly** ['ʃiːpɪʃli] stupidly, foolishly – 18 **to even it up** to make things equal – 20 **to beat sb to sth (beat, beaten)** [biːt biːtən] to be ahead of sb, to realize a plan before sb else – 21 **dough** [dəʊ] *(slang)* money – 22 **dicks** *(AE, slang)* police – 24 **to toss** to throw – 26 **to trudge** [trʌdʒ] to walk heavily

It stopped in front of a brick building with barred windows.

"Harvey," he said to the waiting driver, "wait here for me. I'll be only a moment."

5 The chauffeur touched his cap respectfully. "Yes, Doctor Vandermoor," he said.

1 brick stone made of baked earth – 3 **Harvey** [ˈhɑːvi] name

Discuss the following questions:

1. What are the dangers in offering hitch-hikers a lift?
2. How did the elderly gentleman react to the hitch-hikers' story? Would you have done the same?
3. What do we learn about the characters of the young men?
4. What do we learn about the character of the elderly gentleman?
5. Why did the slim man change his mind and tear the check into pieces?
6. What would have happened if the young man had kept the check?
7. Do you think that the elderly gentleman was mad or not? How do you know?

4. Suspicion of Murder

by William C. Ford

Grimlock was only a spectator at the inquest. He had come only for pleasure, for he had hated Bedoff.
5 Besides that, he wanted to see what was going to happen to Melis who was suspected of the murder. He rather liked young Melis. He could follow instructions, and Grimlock had used him sometimes for that reason, and because he had no conscience.
10 But he was no leader. Grimlock used him like the others as little as possible. It was no good having too many people familiar with his business. In the great courtroom, the old Judge sat high on the bench, with his robes around him. It made quite a scene. Lots of
15 dignity they threw into these inquests; and it impressed the people.

As if there wasn't all that pulling and hauling behind the scenes. Grimlock could pull and haul as well as the best of them. That was his strong point, or one of
20 his strong points. That's what he was there for.

Nothing very bad was going to happen to young Melis. Grimlock had seen to that. They would take care of it some way. Just how – Grimlock didn't know yet. He generally left details like that to his well paid
25 tools. He would enjoy seeing things develop as the hearing went on.

---

1 **suspicion** [səsˈpɪʃn] *here*: feeling that sb is a criminal – 3 **Grimlock** [ˈgrɪmlɒk] name –
3 **inquest** [[ˈɪŋkwest] official hearing in a law-court, an inquiry into a death – 4 **Bedoff**
[beˈdɒf] name – 6 **Melis** [ˈmelis] name – 6 **to suspect sb of a murder** [səsˈpekt] to think
that sb is a murderer – 9 **conscience** [ˈkɒnʃənts] sb's inner voice telling him whether
he is doing right or wrong – 12 **to be familiar with sth** [fəˈmɪliə] to know all about
sth – 14 **robes** [rəʊbz] coat-like clothing worn as a sign of high rank – 15 **dignity**
[ˈdɪgnəti] ceremony, high respect – 17 **to haul** [hɔːl] to pull with force – 18 **all that**
pulling and hauling behind the scenes [siːnz] things being influenced by people
outside the law-court – 25 **tools** [tuːlz] *here*: men following their boss's orders blindly

Bedoff had died suddenly. On the ship it was. The great *Balkania,* just after she had docked at the port in the Far East where Grimlock was powerful. So many things were going on as that great ship had moved
5 into the dock. War or Peace! It was all to be decided so soon.

Bedoff might have chosen peace, and peace wasn't what Grimlock had been working for right then. Not till those armaments were sold, anyway. And Grimlock
10 hated Bedoff. Everybody knew that. And everybody knew that nothing stopped Grimlock when he was crossed. Why hadn't that fool Bedoff stayed away, instead of shouldering in with his gold? Well, he had paid for it. And now Bedoff was dead. Choked they
15 said. And they were whispering this and that of the various agents of Grimlock. Suspicion, that was it. Not much to go on, but whispers, whispers everywhere. And they were suspecting young Melis more than anyone else. Just because he was one of those who
20 were close to Grimlock, probably, and just because the description of the man who had been seen coming out of Bedoff's stateroom fitted Melis – as it fitted a lot of others sitting there in that courtroom. Melis sat there too, calm, quiet, confident.

25 The evidence proceeded slowly. Bedoff, it seemed, had been found in his bunk on the ship, just after she had docked. There had been marks on the throat as if he had been choked. The description of the man who had been seen when leaving Bedoff's stateroom

---

2 **Balkania** [bɔːlˈkeɪnɪə] name of a ship – 3 **Far East** *here:* a part of New York –
9 **armaments** [ˈɑːməmənts] weapons like guns, pistols, etc – 12 **when he was crossed**
when sb annoyed him, made him angry – 13 **to shoulder in** [ˈʃəʊldəˈrin] to force one's
way into other people's business – 14 **to choke sb** [tʃəʊk] to kill sb by pressing his
throat and stopping his breathing – 22 **stateroom** [ˈsteitrʊm] private cabin –
24 **confident** [ˈkɒnfidənt] feeling certain of what will happen – 25 **evidence** [ˈevɪdənts]
what people say at an inquest – 26 **bunk** narrow bed on a ship (usually fixed to the
wall)

was so indefinite that it might have been anybody. The first success for Grimlock's power!

The testimony went on. There were things against young Melis. Grimlock had known that. His alibi, for instance. It seemed to have been neglected, terribly neglected, for there were gaps. It would have been so easy to have cared for all that before the inquest began. Grimlock frowned; and when he frowned, the Honourable Court, the Learned Prosecutor, the Medical Examiner, and others felt uneasy.

The testimony went slowly on. The Government doctor was coming to the stand. Medical Examiner he was. Yes, he had performed the autopsy. Yes, the neck was swollen – and the face. Yes, that was consistent with violent death. Yes, by strangulation. Entirely consistent.

Grimlock frowned again. The doctor went on. "But," said the doctor, "all those symptoms were also consistent with something else."

Grimlock relaxed. His boys had seen to it. Whatever it was, it was coming now.

"Proceed," the Presiding Judge said.

And the witness continued.

"In a normal case," he said, "we would have reached a conclusion of murder by strangulation."

---

1 **indefinite** [ɪnˈdefɪnət] not exact, not clear – 3 **testimony** [ˈtestɪmənɪ] statements by people in court – 4 **alibi** [ˈælɪbaɪ] statement that one was in another place at the time of a crime – 5 **to neglect sth** [nɪˈglekt] to pay no attention to sth, to be careless about sth – 6 **gaps** unfilled places, *here*: gaps of time (the alibi is not perfect) – 8 **to frown** [fraʊn] to draw one's eyebrows together, to look grim – 9 **the Learned Prosecutor** [ˈlɜːnɪd ˈprɒsɪkjuːtə] sb who has studied law and makes inquiries for the State – 12 **stand** *here*: a box in the law-court where people have to stand when they are examined – 13 **to perform** [pəˈfɔːm] **an autopsy** [ˈɔːtɒpsɪ] to examine a dead body – 14 **to swell (swelled, swollen)** [ˈswəʊlən] to become (grow) thick – 15 **to be consistent with sth** [kənˈsɪstənt] to be in agreement with sth, to fit sth – 15 **violent** [ˈvaɪələnt] by force – 15 **strangulation** [stræŋɡjʊˈleɪʃn] choking – 18 **symptom** [ˈsɪmptəm] a sign typical of sth, *here*: of an illness – 20 **to relax** [rɪˈlæks] to take things easy, to feel better – 22 **to proceed** [prəʊˈsiːd] *here*: to go on speaking – 23 **witness** [ˈwɪtnəs] sb who knows sth (who has seen sth happen) and who is expected to tell the truth about it – 25 **to reach a conclusion** [kənˈkluːʒən] to come to an end; to come to a decision

He looked at Melis, with a side glance at Grimlock. He was beginning to enjoy his role.

"But," he said again, "we did not reach that conclusion. We had received a most alarming confidential message from Cairo just before we went into that stateroom. It was the tourist season, and for that reason the news had been suppressed. But as the ship had left Cairo only eight days earlier and because of the very great danger, they had informed us – confidentially of course."

"Go on," ordered the Prosecutor. And he, too, stole a look at Grimlock. Pretty clever, he thought. And true, too, which was almost as good. Maybe this was going to be the making of him. He leaned back for the answer.

The doctor took a deep breath.

"Plague had broken out in Cairo," he said.

"Exactly the incubation period of eight days had passed since the *Balkania* had left Cairo. That changed our opinion ..." Grimlock leaned forward again.

"How does the plague develop?" the Prosecutor asked.

"The first indication," said the doctor, relaxing now, "is a lump or tumor, no larger than a walnut, to be felt beneath the armpit. That is the first thing to look for. You can feel it with the hand. It develops eight days after exposure. After it has developed, nothing can save the patient."

---

2 **role** [rəʊl] an actor's part in a play – 5 **confidential** [kɒnfɪ'dentʃl] **message** ['mesɪdʒ] secret news – 5 **Cairo** ['kaɪrəʊ] town in Egypt ['i:dʒɪpt] – 7 **to suppress sth** [sə'pres] *here*: to keep sth a secret – 14 **to be the making of sb** to lead to sb's success – 17 **plague** [pleɪg] pestilence, a deadly illness that spreads quickly – 18 **incubation period** [ɪnkjʊ'beɪʃn 'pɪəriəd] the time during which an infection can be given to others – 23 **indication** [ɪndɪ'keɪʃn] sign, symptom – 24 **lump, tumor** ['tju:mə] part of the body that begins growing (swelling) in an unnatural way – 25 **armpit** ['ɑ:mpɪt] that part of the body where shoulder and arm come together – 27 **exposure** [ɪks'pəʊʒə] *here*: the moment sb gets into contact with a sick person

"Go on, doctor," said the Prosecutor.

"Shortly after the lump appears," the witness went on, "nausea follows, with some perspiring and fever."

5 "Proceed, doctor," said the Prosecutor.

"In a few hours there is pain in the abdomen, accompanied by a swelling of the throat and face. The face is distorted as by strangulation. Death follows shortly."

10 "Do you think it possible," the Prosecutor asked, and now he was talking very slowly and looking at the Magistrate, "that the deceased may have caught the plague in Cairo?"

"I think it not only possible, but surely true," said 15 the doctor. "All the symptoms were those of death by plague. We found out that the deceased left the ship for an hour at Cairo. He would have needed only to touch with his bare hands the naked skin of a person infected, and the plague would have been transmitted. 20 Personal contact, together possibly with bringing the face within five or six feet of the face of the sick person so as to catch the breath is enough."

The Prosecutor spoke softly. "You took, of course, all necessary precautions for the safety of the 25 public?"

The doctor went on.

"We took all possible precautions immediately, of course. Everything was disinfected and the stateroom was locked. Because of the tourist season we didn't 30 tell anybody until now – since all danger is now

---

3 **nausea** [ˈnɔːsiə] sick feeling – 3 **to perspire** [pəˈspaiə] to sweat, to get wet all over one's body – 6 **abdomen** [ˈæbdəmən] the middle part of the body with the stomach inside – 8 **to distort** [dɪˈstɔːt] to twist, to pull out of the usual form – 12 **Magistrate** [ˈmædʒɪstreɪt] a judge in a police-court – 12 **deceased** [dɪˈsiːst] a dead man or woman – 19 **to transmit** [trænsˈmɪt] to spread, to pass on – 24 **precaution** [prɪˈkɔːʃn] care taken in advance to avoid danger

passed. This was by order of the Government. It is eight days since his death. If anyone had been exposed, the first symptom would have appeared by this time. As far as we know, however, no one was
5 exposed by coming in contact with him at the acute stage. We don't believe the indefinite claims as to seeing a person leave the stateroom."

"And your final conclusion, doctor?" asked the Prosecutor, smiling.

10 "That he came to his death by the plague, and that no one may be accused of violence toward him," said the witness, emphatically.

"You may step down," said the Prosecutor, and he bowed to the Court.

15 "I cannot ask for further inquest," he said.

Grimlock was cleared! No one could be suspected now. Bedoff was disposed of ! True, Bedoff would have died anyway, and in agony. But all was well – Grimlock shrugged.

20 No elation! Never had Grimlock's face been allowed to show his feelings, never in his life. Showing nothing! That was it. He hardly saw the bow of the Medical Examiner or the dignified nod of the Magistrate. He hardly knew that he returned them.

25 No elation! No feeling! He had won again – as always. He pushed through the crowd. Were they wondering a bit at his haste? Slowly!

---

6 **acute stage** [əˈkjuːt ˈsteɪdʒ] dangerous period – 6 **claims** [kleɪmz] *here*: statements (what people say) – 12 **to say sth emphatically** [ɪmˈfætɪkli] to stress one's words – 14 **to bow** [baʊ] to bend one's body or head forward – 17 **to be disposed** [dɪsˈpəʊzd] **of** to be got out of the way, to be got rid of – 18 **agony** [ˈægəni] great pain, death-struggle – 19 **to shrug** [ʃrʌg] *here*: to lift one's shoulders – 20 **elation** [ɪˈleɪʃn] excitement, joy

He walked to the door, smiling now – but the smile set stiff on his face.

And in the corridor, he slipped his hand quietly down inside his coat and under his arm.

5   The lump was there.

Discuss the following questions:

1. How did Bedoff die? Try to reconstruct things as they really happened.
2. What do you think of the Medical Examiner's report?
3. What role did Melis play?
4. What characteristics have all gangsters in common?
5. What power and influence do they exert on public life?
6. What impressed you most with regard to the behaviour of the law-court officials?
7. Should international armament-trading be controlled? If so, by whom?
8. Should the public be informed and warned in a plague case? Or do you see any good reasons for keeping such a plague a secret?
9. What is the significance of the last sentence?

Question 1 **to reconstruct** [riːkənˈstrʌkt] to build or put together again –
Question 9 **significance** [sɪgˈnɪfɪkənts] meaning, importance

5. Written in Fire

by Florence McIntyre

It was mid-winter and Mrs. Durkin's two-family house was cold and cheerless.

5 "You ought to turn on a little heat, Mom," said young Mike as he sat in the kitchen of their downstairs apartment. Though Mike called Mrs. Durkin 'Mom', she was not his mother. Some years ago – quite a few – when his parents had been killed in an accident, it

10 was natural that he should go to live with his father's widowed sister. It was not only natural, but necessary, for there was nobody else. Mrs. Durkin did not like the new burden, but there was not much she could do about it.

15 Mrs. Durkin looked up from the pan of potatoes which she was peeling. "You should try to get used to the cold," she declared. "You'll be in the Army any day now. Suppose you land in Russia or up where those Japs are?"

20 "I don't mind," said Mike. "I can stand cold, but what about that kid upstairs? You know the boy has been sick, and a chill may put him back in bed again. The government doesn't ask anybody to freeze."

Mike knew very well that it was not patriotism that

25 made his aunt save fuel. She had never been a generous woman. That is why Mike had so little schooling. When he was sixteen, she got the working

---

3 **Mrs. Durkin** [ˈdɜːkɪn] name – 4 **cheerless** [ˈtʃɪələs] unpleasant, unfriendly – 6 **Mike** [maɪk] short for Michael [ˈmaɪkl] – 9 **accident** [ˈæksɪdənt] sth bad that happens by chance (for example when two cars run into each other) – 11 **widowed woman** [ˈwɪdəʊd] woman whose husband is dead – 13 **burden** [ˈbɜːdn] heavy load, difficult task – 19 **Japs** [dʒæps] *(slang)* Japanese [dʒæpəˈniːz] – 21 **kid** *(slang)* child – 22 **chill** unpleasant feeling of coldness – 23 **to freeze** [friːz] to feel very cold – 25 **fuel** [ˈfjʊəl] material for burning like coal, oil, etc

papers for him and placed him with the grocer where she traded. Mike never knew the thrill of opening his pay envelope. 'Mom' did it for him. But despite the handicaps, Mike had made progress. Through the free night technical school he had become an electrician and now was earning good wages. And it was the loss of his very generous weekly stipend to her – when the Army should claim him – which tore bitterly at the old woman's heart. There had been stormy scenes between them as 'Mom' Durkin insisted that Mike should claim her as his dependent and stay on his job.

Mike said "No". If his country needed him and called him, he was willing to go – just like any other young man. And now within ten days he would be in the Army.

'Mom' also bitterly opposed Mike's wish to marry Ann Quinn, a nice girl, daughter of a neighbour, whom they both had long known. As time grew short, Mike was more than ever determined to marry Ann for he was sure that even ten days of life together would give them something 'grand', no matter what else might happen. That is why he had written to Ann so ardently. That is why he so desperately awaited a reply to his letter, a letter in which he had poured out his young heart. Ann, too, had answered her country's call. She was a volunteer student nurse in a great Baltimore hospital. Mike could imagine her in her white uniform, moving about the ward – lovely, radiant, vital Ann

---

2 **thrill** [θrɪl] an exciting feeling – 4 **handicap** ['hændikæp] *here*: lack of freedom –
7 **generous stipend** ['dʒenərəs 'staɪpənd] *here*: a large sum of money given away freely – 8 **to claim** to declare, to state sth as a fact – 8 **to tear** [teə] **(tore, torn)** [tɔː tɔːn] *here*: to pull – 11 **dependent** [dɪ'pendənt] relative who needs the help of another person (his money, food, etc) – 18 **Ann Quinn** ['æn 'kwɪn] name – 22 **grand** splendid, most beautiful – 23 **ardently** ['ɑːdntli] wishfully, in a desiring way – 27 **volunteer** [vɒlən'tɪə] of one's own free will – 27 **Baltimore** ['bɔːltɪmɔː] town in the USA – 29 **ward** [wɔːd] part (division) of a hospital – 29 **radiant** ['reɪdiənt] looking bright and lovely, beaming – 29 **vital** ['vaɪtl] *here*: full of life and energy

who brought joy to all who saw her smile. But – why hadn't she answered his letter? Why? There were only ten days left!

Glancing up from his newspaper, Mike looked suspiciously at his aunt.

"Are you sure, Mom," he asked, "there hasn't been a letter for me this week?"

"None that I have seen," she said looking him straight in the eye. "And if it is that girl in Baltimore you are wanting to hear from – why, lad, she has probably forgotten all about you. New faces, new fancies!" She laughed her short, hard laugh.

Mrs. Durkin was lying to the boy. Cruelly, deliberately lying to him. The letter from Ann had come; the letter telling him that she would marry him – any day; telling him where and when to telephone her for further discussion of their plans. Yes, Mrs. Durkin had made short work of that letter after she had read it again and again. But she did follow through by making a telephone call to Ann, herself.

"Yes, dearie," she had told the astonished girl, "Mike is in the Army now. He'll probably write to you when he gets set ... but you know, dearie, those soldier boys – new faces, new fancies!"

The old woman smiled maliciously as she put the telephone receiver back onto its hook. "Any Army pay that is coming to a dependent is coming to me."

Now she was sitting there opposite Mike, knitting and thinking over the whole scene. She watched him slyly from the corner of her eye. Big, shaggy, red-

---

5 **suspiciously** [səsˈpɪʃəsli] showing doubt and distrust – 12 **fancies** [ˈfæntsiz] *here*: wishes, desires – 13 **deliberately** [dɪˈlɪbrətli] on purpose, following a plan – 19 **to follow through** *here*: to complete things, to make things perfect – 23 **when he gets set** when he has got the time, when he knows where he is to stay – 25 **malicious** [məˈlɪʃəs] with ill will, like sb who is planning bad things – 30 **slyly** [ˈslaɪli] secretly – 30 **shaggy** [ˈʃægi] rough-haired, with untidy hair

headed Mike was in love all right – and suffering. But he was young. He would get over it. Mike rose to pace the kitchen floor. "Anything to eat?" he asked. "It's after six o'clock."

5 "Ham and cabbage, fit for a king." Mrs. Durkin began spreading the table, and then somebody knocked at the door. In a flash, Bobby, the eight-year-old boy from upstairs, entered the room. "Mrs. Durkin," he began politely, "my Mama just phoned
10 that she'll be late getting home from work. She says if you please give me my supper, she will pay for it tomorrow."

"Sure," said Mike, his face beaming at the youngster, "you're our guest of honour."

15 "Of course, I'll feed you, Bobby," said Mrs. Durkin, "and your Mama won't have to pay for it either – for you are going to earn your own supper!"

"What must I do?"

"Just run down to the cellar and gather up all the
20 old papers and rags. Where's the string" – she handed it to him –"tie them all up nice and neat, and tomorrow we'll sell them to the junk man." Mike was too disgusted to say a word. After some time Bobby returned.

25 "Gee," said Mike, beckoning to the lad, "I'll bet your hands are dirty ..." But then his breath stopped suddenly. In one small dirty fist Bobby held a letter, a scorched letter directed to Mike in Ann's handwriting! Mike tore it open. "Where did you get this, kid?"

---

1 **to suffer** ['sʌfə] to feel pain or sorrow – 2 **to pace** [peɪs] to take steps, to go to and fro – 5 **cabbage** ['kæbɪdʒ] kind of green vegetable – 7 **Bobby** short for Robert ['rɒbət] – 20 **rags** [rægz] pieces of old and worn clothes – 21 **neat** [niːt] tidy, orderly – 22 **junk** [dʒʌŋk] things of little value, rubbish – 23 **to be disgusted** [dɪsˈgʌstɪd] to feel shocked, to have a strong feeling of dislike – 25 **Gee** [dʒiː] *(slang)* Jesus – 25 **to beckon to sb** ['bekən] to give sb a sign to come nearer – 25 **I'll bet** *here*: I'm sure – 28 **to scorch** [skɔːtʃ] to burn sth or take away the colour of sth by heating it

"Out of the furnace," Bobby told him frankly. "The fire was out, so I took it because I wanted that stamp."

Mike's tone was furious as he surveyed his aunt. "This is the letter I've been waiting for. How did it get into the furnace?"

"Well, now, I don't know, Mike." The old woman's face was twisting. She wetted her lips and tried to go on. "Unless Bobby ...", she gulped, "took it from the postman and ..."

"The hell he did," Mike roared as he went to the hall, shrugged into his coat and slapped on his hat.

"Good-bye, Mom," he called back, "I'll be seeing you – maybe with my wife – sometime after the war."

---

1 **furnace** [ˈfɜːnɪs] fireplace for central heating – 3 **to survey** [səˈveɪ] *here*: to watch sb carefully, to examine sb – 7 **to twist** to turn round, to move – 8 **to gulp** [gʌlp] to swallow quickly – 10 **the hell he did** he didn't do anything like that; this is not true – 10 **to roar** [rɔː] to make loud, deep sounds like lions – 11 **to shrug into sth** [ʃrʌg] *here*: to put sth on carelessly – 11 **to slap** to give sth a quick blow with the flat hand

Discuss the following questions:

1. *What type of woman is Mrs. Durkin?*
2. *Would you say that her attitude towards Mike can be understood in a way, as she did not like "that burden"?*
3. *She does not only hurt the feelings of others, but also disregards the laws of the country. In what way?*
4. *What would you have done in Mike's place?*
5. *Should apprentices hand over their pay envelopes to their parents or foster-parents as a rule?*
6. *What would you have done in Ann's place after receiving such a telephone call?*
7. *Why is little Bobby's case so typical of many children of our time?*
8. *What impressed you most when reading this story?*

Question 2 **attitude** ['ætɪtjuːd] way of feeling or thinking –
Question 3 **to disregard** to take no notice of, to ignore –
Question 5 **apprentice** [ə'prentɪs] a young person who is learning a trade –
foster-parent sb who looks after a child but who is not one of the
child's parents